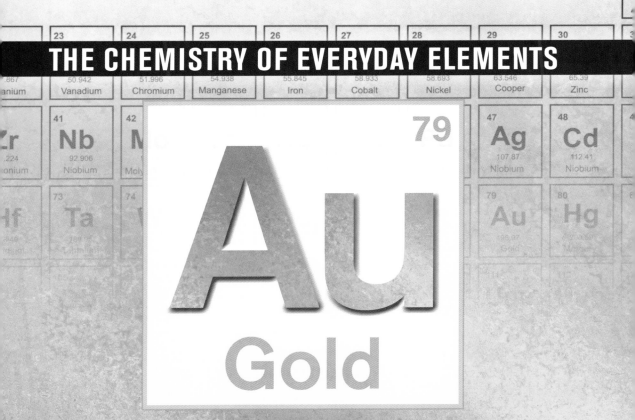

THE CHEMISTRY OF EVERYDAY ELEMENTS

23		24		25		26		27		28		29		30	
.867		50.942		51.996		54.938		55.845		58.933		58.693		63.546		65.39
anium		Vanadium		Chromium		Manganese		Iron		Cobalt		Nickel		Cooper		Zinc

41	42		47	48
Nb	**M**		**Ag**	**Cd**
92.906			107.87	112.41
Niobium	Moly		Niobium	Niobium

73	74		79	80
Ta			**Au**	**Hg**
			196.97	
			Gold	

79

Au
Gold

Mason Crest

THE CHEMISTRY OF EVERYDAY ELEMENTS

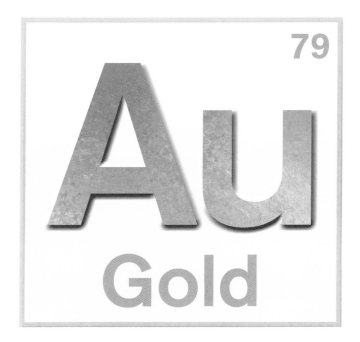

By Kathryn Hulick

Mason Crest
450 Parkway Drive, Suite D
Broomall, PA 19008
www.masoncrest.com

Printed and bound in the United States of America.

Series ISBN: 978-1-4222-3837-0
Hardback ISBN: 978-1-4222-3840-0
EBook ISBN: 978-1-4222-7945-8

First printing
1 3 5 7 9 8 6 4 2

Produced by Shoreline Publishing Group LLC
Santa Barbara, California
Editorial Director: James Buckley Jr.
Designer: Patty Kelley
www.shorelinepublishing.com

Library of Congress Cataloging-in-Publication Data on file with the Publisher.

Cover photographs by NASA (2); Björn Wylezich/Dreamstime.com (coins).

QR Codes disclaimer:

You may gain access to certain third party content ("Third-Party Sites") by scanning and using the QR Codes that appear in this publication (the "QR Codes"). We do not operate or control in any respect any information, products, or services on such Third-Party Sites linked to by us via the QR Codes included in this publication, and we assume no responsibility for any materials you may access using the QR Codes. Your use of the QR Codes may be subject to terms, limitations, or restrictions set forth in the applicable terms of use or otherwise established by the owners of the Third-Party Sites. Our linking to such Third-Party Sites via the QR Codes does not imply an endorsement or sponsorship of such Third-Party Sites, or the information, products, or services offered on or through the Third- Party Sites, nor does it imply an endorsement or sponsorship of this publication by the owners of such Third-Party Sites.

KEY ICONS TO LOOK FOR

Words to Understand: These words with their easy-to-understand definitions will increase the reader's understanding of the text, while building vocabulary skills.

Sidebars: This boxed material within the main text allows readers to build knowledge, gain insights, explore possibilities, and broaden their perspectives by weaving together additional information to provide realistic and holistic perspectives.

Educational Videos: Readers can view videos by scanning our QR codes, providing them with additional educational content to supplement the text. Examples include news coverage, moments in history, speeches, iconic moments, and much more!

Text-Dependent Questions: These questions send the reader back to the text for more careful attention to the evidence presented here.

Research Projects: Readers are pointed toward areas of further inquiry connected to each chapter. Suggestions are provided for projects that encourage deeper research and analysis.

Series Glossary of Key Terms: This back-of-the-book glossary contains terminology used throughout this series. Words found here increase the reader's ability to read and comprehend higher-level books and articles in this field.

Striking Gold

ook around. What do you see? Maybe your pet cat or yesterday's lunch dishes or that book you're supposed to read for English class. Outside your window, you might see a car rolling by or a tree losing its leaves. What do you feel? Your breath travels in and out, filling your lungs, while your heart pumps blood around your body. All of those things—the solids, liquids, and gases around you and inside you—are composed of elements of the periodic table.

WORDS TO UNDERSTAND

corrode   to damage or weaken gradually through a chemical reaction

isotope   an atom of a specific element that has a different number of neutrons; it has the same atomic number but a different atomic mass

The periodic table is an arrangement of all the naturally occurring, and manufactured, elements known to humans at this point in time. An element is a substance that cannot be broken down into simpler chemical substances. Ninety-two

To most people, gold is the most valuable and well-known element.

elements occur naturally on Earth and in space. Twenty-six more elements (and counting) have been manufactured and analyzed in a laboratory setting. These elements, alone or in combination with others, form and shape all the matter around us. From the air we breathe, to the water we drink, to the bananas we eat—all these things are made of elements.

These elements are organized into a chart called the periodic table. Since it was first developed in 1869, the periodic table went through several updates and reorganizations until it became the modern version of the table used today. On it, each square represents a single element. These elements are arranged into rows and columns by increasing atomic number. The atomic number equals the number of

**79**
Au
Gold

protons in the nucleus of the atom. Each element has a unique atomic number. Gold has an atomic number of 79 because it has 79 protons in its nucleus. The nucleus of an atom may also contain neutrons. When an atom has the same number of protons as an element on the chart, but a different number of neutrons, it is called an **isotope**.

Each element on the periodic table has its own unique chemical and physical properties. The chart helps keep track of elements with certain chemical properties by arranging them into columns, groups, or rows. In addition to the atomic number, each square in the periodic table also lists the name of the element and its chemical symbol (Au for gold), along with other important information such as the number of neutrons in the nucleus of one atom of an element, the number of electrons that surround the nucleus, the atomic mass, and the general size of the atom. The periodic table is a very useful tool as one begins to investigate chemistry and science in general. (For lots more on the periodic table, read *Understanding the Periodic Table*, another book in this series.)

This book is about the element gold. Its name comes from the Anglo-Saxon word for gold, *aurum*. Humans have recognized the beauty and uniqueness of this shiny yellow metal since ancient times.

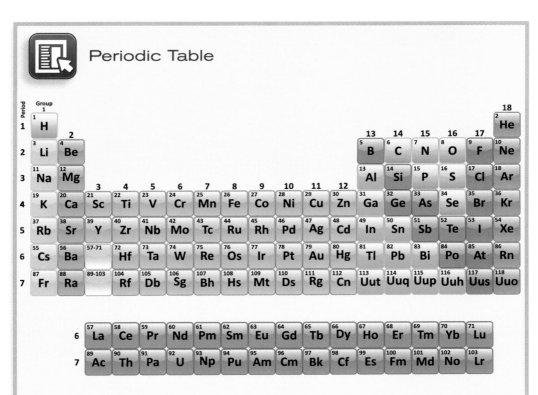

Periodic Table

The Periodic Table of the Elements is arranged in numerical order. The number of each element is determined by the number of protons in its nucleus. The horizontal rows are called periods. The number of the elements increases across a period, from left to right. The vertical columns are called groups. Groups of elements share similar characteristics. The colors, which can vary depending on the way the creators design their version of the chart, also create related collections of elements, such as noble gases, metals, or nonmetals, among others.

Gold's durable physical properties make it ideal for use in satellites.

Almost every single human culture, from ancient Egypt and the Inca Empire to modern America, has prized gold and used it for various purposes, including jewelry, art, decoration, and as a unit of currency. Gold was one of nine elements known to ancient cultures. The others were silver, copper, iron, tin, lead, mercury, carbon, and sulfur.

Gold's allure stems from the fact that unlike other metals, gold does not rust or tarnish. As long as the gold is pure, it will remain shiny and lustrous forever. Although gold is not the rarest or even the most valuable metal, it is surely one of the most famous. Gold has built empires and lured explorers to conquer new lands. People have fought wars to gain access to gold. First place in the Olympics earns a gold medal. A person who suddenly becomes rich or successful has "struck gold." Something very useful can be said to be "worth its weight in gold."

But gold is more than just shiny loot. It can be stretched and hammered into extremely thin sheets or wires. Gold conducts electricity and doesn't **corrode** (which means to break apart slowly), so engineers often use it to form components of computer chips and other electronics. That cell phone sitting on the table contains about $1 to $2 worth of gold. Gold also has medical applications. Dentists often use gold to fill in cavities. Gold has also helped treat arthritis and cancer. Gold is even useful in outer space, where it helps shield spacecraft and coats the mirrors on a giant space telescope.

Despite the many technical uses for gold, the metal remains valuable mainly for its beauty and rarity. In almost any time and place on Earth, gold is an acceptable form of payment.

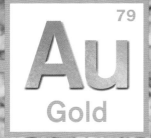

Au 79

Gold

Discovery and History

Gold is a relatively rare element, and that rarity is one of the things that makes it so desirable. If you rank all of the elements by their abundance on Earth, gold comes in 73rd place. The elements platinum, osmium, rhodium, and iridium are all more rare and more expensive, but gold is one of the few elements that people have fought, killed, and died for throughout history.

Earth's supply of gold probably arrived here during an asteroid bombardment nearly four billion years ago. These gold atoms originally formed in space, likely when **neutron stars** collided. Most of the gold on Earth is spread out, showing up at extremely low concentrations inside of seawater, plants, animals, rocks, and soil. However, volcanic activity, earthquakes,

Au 79
Gold

and heat and pressure inside Earth can lead to the buildup of gold in certain areas. Gold has most often been found along with quartz in veins of rock or deposited in streambeds.

Many early human civilizations came across nuggets of gold and formed objects from the soft, yellow metal. Though gold is too soft to make tools or weapons, it is easy to work with and doesn't corrode. These qualities made it a perfect material for jewelry, crowns, symbolic statues or religious objects, and for coins and other units of currency.

Archaeologists have unearthed gold objects dating from as long as 6,000 years ago. In 2600 BCE, the Sumerian people, who lived in an area that is now part of Iraq, buried gold jewelry, bowls, daggers, and other objects alongside their kings and queens. The ancient Egyptians found gold in the Nile River, and later started mining for gold. By 2500 BCE, Egyptians had mastered the art of filigree, or forming gold into a thin wire that is then twisted to form designs. The coffin of the famous pharaoh Tutankhamun

Ancient gold mining

Golden Tales

Due to gold's importance in so many civilizations, it should come as no surprise that gold plays a central role in numerous stories. In one tale, King Midas wished that everything he touched would turn to gold. Unfortunately, that meant he couldn't drink or eat anything, and he had to ask for his "golden touch" to be taken away. In

Greek mythology, the hero Jason searched for the Golden Fleece. It hung from a tree guarded by a dragon. In a German fairy tale, a small man named Rumpelstiltskin gave a young girl the ability to spin straw into gold. One of Aesop's fables told of a goose that laid golden eggs. Gold is mentioned numerous times in the Bible, including this passage from the Book of Kings: "All King Solomon's drinking vessels were of gold, and all the vessels of the House of the Forest of Lebanon were of pure gold."

(King Tut), who died in 1323 BCE, is inlaid with 220 pounds (100 kg) of gold. Civilizations in South America, including the Chavin and the Nazca, both located in what is now Peru, also valued gold and worked it into various shapes and designs.

This display includes tools of the alchemist's trade.

The Philosopher's Stone

Because gold was so rare and valuable, some sought to find a way to produce it and other substances through chemical reactions. These kinds of experiments began with the Egyptians and continued with Greek and Arab scholars. By the eighth century, Arab scholars had brought the practice to Spain. These experiments came to be known as **alchemy**, and flourished in the Middle Ages in Europe.

Independently, alchemists in China and India searched for potions that could prolong a person's life or even bestow immortality. In the fourth century, a Chinese alchemist named Ko

The tomb of King Tut revealed amazing gold artifacts, such as this full-body sarcophagus of the "boy king."

Hung wrote: "When gold enters the flames, even after one hundred firings, it will not disappear. If you bury it forever, it will never decay." He went on to say that ingesting gold could give a person those same qualities; the person would not grow older or die.

To alchemists in Europe, gold was seen as the perfect metal, and equated with the sun. Other metals could supposedly be turned to gold with a magical substance called the philosopher's stone. This stone would also make a person immortal. Of course, the alchemists did not find such a stone. Gold is an element, and can't be created or destroyed through chemical reactions. Yet many tried, and some claimed success.

A 15th-century Italian alchemist named Bernard Trevisan set a mixture of silver and mercury out in sunlight, hoping to create gold.

Au ⁷⁹

Gold

Eureka!

One day in ancient Greece, a scholar named Archimedes leapt from his bath and ran naked through the streets, shouting, "Eureka! Eureka!" The word "eureka" means "I've found it," and today it's commonly used to describe a moment of insight or inspiration. As the story goes, Archimedes had been tasked with determining if the king's newly made crown was pure gold, or gold mixed with silver.

Gold is heavier than silver, so a gold and silver crown would have to be thicker, or have more volume, than an object of pure gold with the same weight. To compare the volumes of these two objects, Archimedes realized that he could place each object in a bowl of water. Just as his own body displaced an amount of water from the bath equal to his size, the crown would displace an amount that gave away its volume. The story ends with Archimedes determining that the crown was, in fact, part silver.

Unfortunately for the history of science, this event probably never happened. Archimedes never wrote about it. The first known telling of the story happened 200 years after his death. In addition, though the water displacement method can work to measure volume, it's not very accurate. Despite the problems with the story, it's still okay to shout "eureka" in a moment of insight.

Science and history museums often have displays of model "philosopher's" stones.

He said, "For does not the sun acting upon and within the earth form the metals? Is not gold merely its beams condensed to yellow solid?" In 1440, King Henry VI of England issued licenses to practice alchemy, and coins were even minted from "gold" produced by a pair of alchemists. But the metal was actually a mixture of mercury, copper, and gold.

Famous scientist Sir Isaac Newton was convinced that gold could be created, and that ancient scholars had succeeded. But he was one of the last to hold onto this belief. Despite the failure of alchemy, the struggle to create gold led to many important scientific discoveries and eventually founded the modern science of chemistry.

Eventually, the alchemist's dream of creating gold from other elements came true. Glenn T. Seaborg, a chemist at Lawrence Berkeley Laboratory in California, transformed bismuth into gold in 1980. The secret was nuclear physics. A particle accelerator can achieve high enough energy to alter the nucleus of an atom. Unfortunately, the cost of making gold this way is much, higher than the value of the gold produced!

Au 79
Gold

Greedy for Gold

The world's first gold coins came from the ancient kingdom of Lydia, which was located in modern-day Turkey. During the 600s BCE, the Lydians began using coins made from **electrum**, a mixture of gold and silver that occurs naturally. By the 500s BCE, pure gold coins entered circulation. The Greek and Roman empires used both gold and silver coins. After the fall of the Roman Empire in the fifth century, European civilizations continued to use coinage made from a range of metals. Gold coins were always the most valuable.

During the age of exploration in the 15th and 16th centuries, Europeans discovered gold in the New World. Spanish armies brought down the mighty Inca Empire and looted its gold and silver. Francisco Pizarro, the leader of the Spanish army, said of his conquest, "I have come to take from them their gold." The Spanish stole a staggering amount of treasure, and they also took over gold and silver mines in the New World. Getting

The Search for El Dorado

A hunger for gold lured numerous explorers to the New World. Francisco Pizarro (right) found what he was looking for and became very rich, at the expense of the native people. Others weren't so successful. Though Christopher Columbus found some natives wearing gold jewelry, he never came across a huge quantity of gold. When Ponce de Leon became the first European in Florida in the 1500s, he was supposedly looking for the Fountain of Youth. More likely, he had his heart set on finding gold. Instead, he was wounded in a fight with Native Americans and died.

Many explorers of the 16th and 17th centuries believed in a mythical "city of gold" that they called El Dorado. Most thought it was located somewhere in the jungles of South America. Gonzalo Pizarro set out into the jungle in 1541 with hundreds of soldiers, thousands of slaves, and many llamas, pigs, and hunting dogs. His expedition was a complete failure. Only 80 men returned alive. Sir Walter Raleigh of England also failed on two separate attempts to find the golden city. He made it back home, only to be beheaded for attacking a Spanish outpost during his travels.

In the 1900s, some explorers were still searching. Percy Fawcett of England disappeared in the South American jungle in 1925. Surprisingly, Fawcett may have been correct about the location of El Dorado. Satellites have found evidence of an ancient city in the area where he was looking. However, it doesn't seem as if the city was actually full of gold.

these precious metals back to Spain wasn't easy. They had to send fleets of warships to protect the precious cargo from pirates.

By the 19th century, paper bills and coins made from common metals began to replace gold and silver money. Yet for a long time, paper bills represented actual gold. From 1880 to 1914, almost all major countries, including England and the United States, adhered to a **gold standard**. This meant that any paper currency could be redeemed for gold. A person would just have to take the bill to a bank and ask for gold in exchange. The United States had to hold huge amounts of gold in reserve to back up this promise.

US currency used to be backed by its weight in gold.

But the system didn't last. With a gold standard in place, a government can't easily adjust the amount of money in the financial system in order to fight a depression or other economic emergency. European countries went off the gold standard during World War I, followed by the United States during the Great Depression in the 1930s. However,

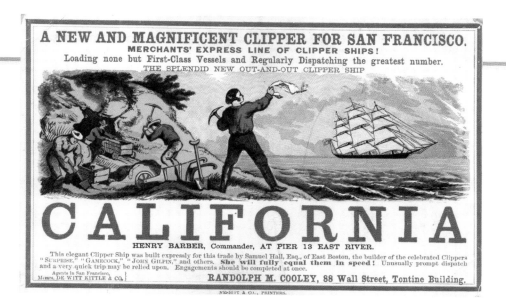

Gold transformed California from a sleepy farm region into a rich American state.

many countries still hold onto gold as a part of their national treasuries, and all nations still accept gold as a form of payment. Most of the United States' gold is stored at Fort Knox in Kentucky.

Gold Rushes

From 1823 through the 1830s, most of the world's gold came from Russia. Miners dug it out of the freezing tundra. But new sources of gold would soon be found. In 1849, a flash of gold in a stream lured fortune seekers to California. John Sutter had struck gold while building a sawmill, and soon thousands of people, nicknamed 49ers, had arrived seeking their fortunes. In 1851, gold was found in the Australian province of Victoria. And this wasn't just gold dust—one nugget

Au 79

Gold

weighed more than 200 pounds (75 kg). Yet another gold rush in the 1890s drew people to the frigid Yukon Territory of northern Canada.

In 1886, a diamond digger discovered gold in South Africa. Unlike the gold rushes in California and Australia, though, this gold was embedded in rocks, and heavy machinery was required to get it out. In 1890, miners there developed the **cyanide** process, a technical innovation that made it possible to get tiny, particle-sized bits of gold out of rocks. Cyanide, a deadly poison, can dissolve gold and separate it from other minerals. Unfortunately, that method is not very environmentally friendly. Currently, scientists are developing safer, cleaner methods. South Africa was the world's leading gold producer for many years. In the past decade, though, several other countries have taken the lead, including China, Australia, Russia again, and the United States.

Deep beneath these buildings is a big South African gold mine.

Current methods to produce gold from ore aren't nearly as magical as the mythical promises of alchemy, or as exciting as pulling nuggets out of a streambed. But gold mines provide a steady supply of the precious metal for jewelry, electronics, and other important uses.

 Text-Dependent Questions

1. Why doesn't the author give credit to a single person as the one who first discovered gold?

2. Why were the alchemists doomed to failure in their quest to produce gold from other substances?

3. What is a "gold standard" in economics?

Research Project

Alchemists made many important scientific discoveries while trying to produce gold. They discovered new compounds, new acids, and even new elements. Research the history of alchemy, and find an example of one of these early discoveries. Describe how the discovery happened, and why it was important in the history of chemistry.

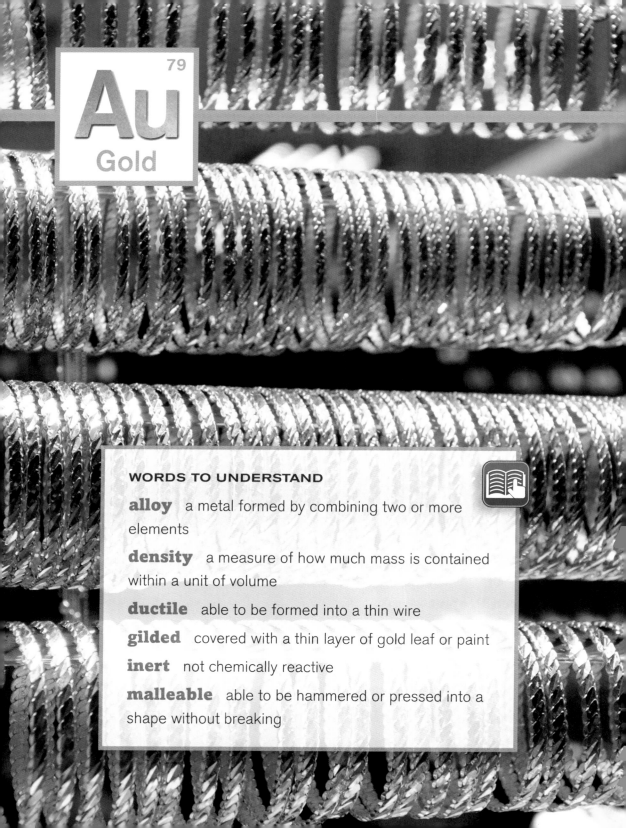

79

Au

Gold

WORDS TO UNDERSTAND

alloy   a metal formed by combining two or more elements

density   a measure of how much mass is contained within a unit of volume

ductile   able to be formed into a thin wire

gilded   covered with a thin layer of gold leaf or paint

inert   not chemically reactive

malleable   able to be hammered or pressed into a shape without breaking

Chemical Properties

O ver time, iron rusts, silver blackens, and copper turns green. These changes all happen due to chemical reactions between the metal and air or other substances. Gold, however, stays shiny and beautiful forever. Any dirt or dust that accumulates on its surface will just wipe off. The yellow metal is almost completely **inert**, meaning that it does not react easily with other elements.

On the periodic table, gold is one of 38 transition metals. Like the rest of this group, gold is **malleable** and **ductile**, meaning that it can be stretched or pulled into thin sheets and wires. It also conducts electricity and reflects light and heat. In addition, gold is very dense.

Au ⁷⁹

Gold

Noble Gold

Gold is noble in more than one way. In addition to being a metal associated with kings and queens, it also does not react easily with other elements.

In the periodic table, gases that do not react easily with other elements or compounds fall into a single column called the "noble gases." The atoms that make up these gases all have a full outer shell of electrons, which is the most stable state for an atom. As a result, they do not easily gain or lose electrons.

The group of noble metals is not so easily defined. Generally, noble metals are any that resist corrosion. These include ruthenium, rhodium, palladium, silver, osmium, iridium, platinum, and gold. Several others may also be included in the list. However, in physics, just copper, silver, and gold are considered noble

Gold is sometimes combined with other metals in coinage.

Gold Leaf

Gold leaf is primarily used in art and design. A **gilded** picture frame, piece of furniture, or domed roof is formed from another material such as wood, then carefully covered with gold leaf. Artisans in early China and medi-eval Europe would even wrap gold leaf around thread or form gold into wires, then embroider clothing or other textiles. Famous Austrian painter Gustav Klimt used gold leaf in many of his paintings, including *The Kiss*.

metals due to the similar structure of the electrons in an atom of each element. Not coincidentally, these three metals are also the three most commonly used throughout history to make coins, because their resistance to corrosion allows them to last a long time. (Silver and copper do tarnish, but can be cleaned.)

In addition, the molecules that make up gold metal form a

structure that resists bonding with other molecules. "The unique role that gold plays in society is to a large extent related to the fact that it is the most noble of all metals; it is the least reactive metal towards atoms or molecules at the interface with a gas or a liquid," wrote the physicists Jens K. Norskov and B. Hammer in an article in the journal *Nature* in 1999. "Even reactive molecules tend to slide away without bonding or affecting gold's surface."

From Gold Wires to Golden Mirrors

While non-reactivity may be gold's most important trait, it also has several other interesting and surprising properties. First of all, gold's high **density** makes the metal extremely heavy. A pure gold bar weighs much more than a steel bar of the same size. The standard gold bars that many banks keep in their vaults are each about the size of a paperback book, but weigh more than 33 pounds (15 kg) each. A steel bar of that size would weigh around 13 pounds (6 kg). Despite this weight difference, fakers still managed to pass off gold-plated steel bars. A bank in Ethiopia discovered they'd been duped that way when they tried to sell the "gold" bars to South Africa.

Bite That Medal

After winning gold in the Olympics, an athlete often bites down on the brand new medal. This is a tradition that harkens back to earlier times when people used actual gold coins as currency. Biting could help a person tell a real gold coin from a fake one. Pure gold is softer than human teeth, so a strong bite would leave a slight mark. Many other metals and minerals are harder. Pyrite, a shiny mineral often called "fool's gold," is hard enough to scratch or damage the teeth.

Olympic medals would fail a real bite test, unfortunately. They are only 1.34 percent gold, and the rest is sterling silver, which is itself a mixture of silver with some copper. When metals are combined like this, the result is called an alloy. In addition to being cheaper to produce, gold **alloys** are almost always harder and more durable than pure gold. Most gold jewelry contains other metals in addition to gold, so it won't scratch or dent as easily as pure gold would.

Au 79

Gold

Gold can be hammered to be very thin sheets or flakes of gold leaf.

Gold is also extremely soft. So soft, that a penny can scratch the surface of pure gold. Gold's density makes the metal relatively easy for artisans to work with. In addition, gold is the most malleable metal. It will keep its shape even when hammered into extremely thin sheets, called gold leaf. A single ounce of gold can form a sheet that covers almost 100 square feet (9 square meters). That sheet, which would be about 400 times thinner than a human hair, would also be large enough to carpet an average-sized room in an American home.

Finally, gold is the most ductile metal, meaning that it can be pulled into a thinner wire than any other metal. A single ounce of gold could be formed into a 50-mile (80 km) golden wire! Gold wire is commonly used in electrical circuits, because of another of gold's important properties. Like most other metals, gold conducts electricity. Silver and copper are better conductors, but gold's higher resistance to corrosion allows circuits made with gold parts to last a long time. While gold allows electricity through with almost no resistance, it reflects both light and heat. That's why gold appears so shiny. Mirrors coated with gold can help reflect light in scientific instruments such as telescopes.

 Text-Dependent Questions

1. What properties make gold a noble metal?

2. What does it mean if a metal is extremely malleable?

3. Why might a person want to make wires out of gold?

Research Project

Weighing a gold bar can help determine if it is real or fake. But the weight test won't work on a really wellmade counterfeit gold bar. Research one other method people can use to ensure that gold objects are actually made of pure gold. Describe how the method works, and which of gold's properties it measures.

Gold and You

You don't have to wear gold earrings or get gold teeth to have gold in your body. Atoms of gold are spread throughout the environment, and some end up inside the human body, mostly in the blood. An adult who weighs 154 pounds (70 kg) has about 0.000007 ounces (0.2 mg) of gold in her body. These bits of gold don't help or hurt. Since gold is inert, it doesn't react with anything. Gold leaf is even used as a fancy garnish on some foods—it's completely safe to eat! Some skin-care products also contain gold, mostly for sparkle. Typically, only very wealthy people can afford to eat gold-garnished food or use gold face creams. But almost everyone interacts with

WORDS TO UNDERSTAND

dermatologist   a doctor who treats skin conditions

electronic waste (e-waste)   discarded computers or other electronic appliances

34

gold on a daily basis. Almost all electronics, from cell phones to televisions, contain tiny gold wires and connectors.

Pass the Gold-Flecked Chocolates

Perhaps nothing flaunts wealth more than eating food decorated with gold. Edible gold comes as a powder, flakes, leaves, or sprinkles. It doesn't taste like anything, or have any nutritional value, but it sure makes food look snazzy. A person with about $50 to spare could spend it on two chocolate truffles coated in pure gold. In Toronto, Canada, $108 buys a pizza garnished with gold leaf. A gold-covered cupcake created for the opening of a new mall in Dubai was valued at $1,010.

Chefs get very inventive with their gold creations. It's possible to dine on sushi wrapped in gold and silver, salad sprinkled with gold flecks, pasta with gold dust, or duck with a gold crust. Eron Novalski, the executive chef at a restaurant in Toronto, Canada, that offers dishes decorated with gold said, "When I studied in France, we used to use a lot of it in pastries, and it's become a trend to augment a dish. The glistening, the flakes—it's almost like fire."

In India, China, and Japan, some foods and drinks contain gold. Eating golden food isn't a new thing, either. The ancient Egyptians believed it was a sacred food. During the Middle Ages, some nobles threw feasts complete with gold-decorated courses. Today, gold food has again become trendy.

Some people even believe that gold has magical healing powers. They may take white powder gold as a supplement or purchase face creams, masks, or lip balms containing gold because they believe it will make their skin healthier. **Dermatologists**, though, caution that gold has never been shown to heal the skin. "At best, [gold face creams] do nothing," said dermatologist Judith Hellman in an interview with *The New York Times*, "and at worst, they can give you irritation of the skin." Indeed, contact with gold gives some people a painful rash.

Electronic Gold

People who don't regularly eat gold-coated chocolates or slather their faces with gold at the spa probably still spend lots of time using a cell phone. That cell phone contains gold, and so does almost every other modern electronic device, from a calculator to a GPS system. Electronic components made from gold may include connectors, contacts, soldered joints, wires, and connection strips. Computer memory chips and microprocessors may also contain gold. While many metals allow electricity to flow through, gold offers the best protection from corrosion.

These electronic components may be tiny, but the amount of gold required by the electronics industry is increasing. Manufacturers around the world used 320 tons of gold (7.7 percent of the world's supply) per year in recent times to make electronic devices, according to United Nations University. That was a big jump from 197 tons in 2001. A single iPhone contains around 0.001 ounce, or 34 mg of gold.

That miniscule amount of gold is worth a little over $1, which doesn't seem like much. But eventually, the phone will get discarded as **electronic waste**, or "e-waste." A pile of e-waste typically contains a higher concentration of gold than the ore in a gold mine. "It takes a ton of ore to get 1 gram of gold," said European Commissioner for the Environment Janez Potocnik in a 2014 speech. "But you can get the same amount from recycling the materials in forty-one mobile phones."

Unfortunately, current e-waste recycling efforts often don't recover very much gold. Most of it ends up in landfills. Experts are working to solve this problem. Stephen Foley, a chemist at the University of Saskatchewan in Canada came up with an acid that can dissolve the gold on an electronic circuit. "Gold is stripped out from circuits in about ten seconds leaving the other metals intact," he said in a press release. Another group of scientists has come up with a way to separate gold from e-waste using mats made of mushrooms.

Before tossing a cell phone or other electronic device, remember that electronics may be the gold mine of the future.

Au 79
Gold

WORDS TO UNDERSTAND

aqua regia a combination of nitric and hydrochloric acids that is highly corrosive

arthritis a medical condition that causes pain and swelling in the joints

karat a measure of gold's purity

nanoparticle a microscopic piece of matter, usually less than 100 nanometers wide

precipitate remove a solid from a liquid solution

Gold Combines

old is an inert, noble metal that does not easily combine with other elements in chemical reactions. But gold does form a few compounds. In addition, gold alloys easily with other metals. An alloy is a mixture of a metal with one or more other elements. Alloys are usually more durable than the metals they are made from.

Aqua Regia: The Water of Kings

Nitric acid dissolves almost all metals, but not gold. For this reason, nitric acid has been used to test gold for authenticity. In 1100, alchemists developed a mixture of nitric and hydrochloric acids that could dissolve gold. They called it *aqua regia*, meaning "king's water." Some chemists today still use aqua

regia to clean beakers and other equipment because it is so strong. Aqua regia is also still an important part of gold refining. Workers use the strong acid to dissolve gold that may have other metals mixed in. The dissolved gold forms a solution called chlorauric acid ($HAuCl_4$). Then, pure gold can be **precipitated** out of the solution.

(In 1940, early in World War II, a chemist used this process to hide Nobel Prize medals from advancing German Nazi forces. Hungarian scientist Georgy de Hevesy, working in a lab in Copenhagen, had been entrusted with the medals awarded to Germans Max von Laue in 1914 and James Franck in 1925 for their work in physics. This defied Nazi orders that no gold could leave Germany. As Nazi forces took over the city of Copenhagen, Hevesy hid the medals by dropping them in aqua

A scientist used gold's properties to save James Franck's Nobel medal.

Red from gold? The element was used in the process that produced this glassware.

regia. "While the invading forces marched in the streets of Copenhagen, I was busy dissolving Laue's and Franck's medals," he wrote in his autobiography. He then stashed the beaker on a shelf. When the war was over, Hevesy returned to the lab to find the beaker untouched. So he precipitated out the gold and sent it to the Nobel foundation. They recreated the medals using that same gold, and gave them back to their rightful owners.)

Chlorauric acid has been used in photography to create images that do not tarnish or fade. In glassmaking, the acid will turn molten glass a rich ruby color. The finished product is called "cranberry glass" or "gold ruby glass." Chlorauric acid has an important modern application, too. It can be used to produce **nanoparticles** of gold. These minuscule bits of gold have a wide range of uses, from medical diagnoses to electronics.

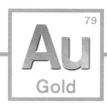

Gold

Purple Gold

Colloidal gold is the name for a liquid (usually water) that contains minute particles of gold called nanoparticles. These nanoparticles change the color of the liquid. Very tiny particles less than 100 nanometers wide result in a bright red solution, while larger particles produce a blue or purple color. The size and shape of the particles affects how they scatter light and also how they conduct electricity. Gold nanoparticles are useful for a wide variety of chemical, biological, medical, and engineering applications.

Other gold compounds include gold(III) chloride, which is sometimes used in reactions in organic chemistry, and gold sodium thiomalate, a medication that helps treat **arthritis**.

Gold Alloys

Unless gold is formed into a bar that will sit in a bank, it almost always contains other metals mixed in. An alloy of gold is formed by melting metals together. When the melted substance solidifies, the

Gold bars and some coins are stamped with their level of gold purity.

molecules of each metal end up distributed evenly, forming a substance that contains gold, but is harder, stronger, or may even be a different color.

The purity of gold is measured in **karats**. Twenty-four-karat gold is 99.99 percent pure, but it's too soft to use for practical purposes. Almost all gold jewelry is actually an alloy of gold with platinum, palladium, silver, copper, or zinc. Eighteen-karat gold is about 75 percent gold. It contains 18 parts gold, and 6 parts of other metals. Ten-karat

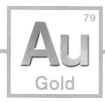

Au 79

Gold

The body of this $400 watch is made of rose gold, made by mixing with copper.

gold is about 40 percent gold, or 10 parts gold and 14 parts metals. This is the minimum amount of gold required for a substance to be called "gold" in the United States. Low-karat gold will tarnish over time because of the other metals mixed in.

Alloys can also change the color of gold. White gold contains palladium or platinum. Rose gold is alloyed with copper. Less common alloys appear purple (gold and aluminum), blue (gold and indium), or black (gold and cobalt).

Text-Dependent Questions

1. What is *aqua regia* used for today?

2. Why is most gold jewelry actually made from a gold alloy?

3. To make rose gold jewelry, what metals would you need to melt together?

Research Project

Neither nitric nor hydrochloric acid can dissolve gold on its own. Yet a combination of these two acids can. Why is that? Research the chemistry behind aqua regia, and describe in your own words why it takes two acids working together to dissolve gold.

Different types of gold

79
Au
Gold

Gold in Our World

Because people have been searching for gold for so long, it's almost impossible to find a new, easily visible gold deposit today. Most modern-day gold miners instead dig up giant truckloads of rocks called ore that contain minute traces of gold. The gold is so scarce inside these rocks that it's impossible to see it with the naked eye. A gold mine today typically contains no visible gold! The ore has to go through an extraction process in order to get the gold out.

In a year, gold mines and gold recycling processes around the world produce about 4,000 tons of gold. Most of the gold, 78 percent, gets made into jewelry. Dental, medical, and electronics applications use up another 12 percent, and the remaining 10 percent is formed into gold bars for financial transactions.

Au 79

Gold

A Real Gold Mine

Today, the leading gold producers in the world are China, Australia, and Russia. But gold almost never comes out of a mine as shiny yellow nuggets. Instead, it is trapped at low concentrations inside rocks. A mine typically recovers about one ounce of gold per ton of rock. But even at that low concentration, the gold is valuable enough to merit the work it takes to remove it.

All the Gold in the Sea

Earth's ocean waters contain quite a lot of gold—about 10 millions tons of it. If someone could extract all that gold, it would be worth as much as $365 trillion. However, the concentration of gold is extremely low. Still, the oceans seemed like a potential gold mine to German chemist Fritz Haber. After its defeat in World War I, Germany owed a huge sum of money. So Haber spent several years working on a method to extract gold from seawater using massive rotating machines called centrifuges. He eventually had to give up when he realized that the amount of energy required to process the seawater would cost more than the gold was worth. Since then, the gold in the sea remains undisturbed.

Smaller gold deposits are found in the form of dust or small nuggets.

There are several different methods for extracting gold from ore. Mercury dissolves gold, so this element can be used to get gold out of rocks. The most popular method, however, is the cyanide process described in Chapter 1. But it's not enough for some stubborn ores. Some mines must first use high temperatures or pressures to remove unwanted minerals from the ore. Even after going through fire, pressure, and cyanide or mercury, gold will not yet be pure.

For centuries, civilizations have known how to separate gold from natural alloys by heating it in a furnace with salt and brick dust. Other metals get burned or absorbed, but the gold remains. A more modern technique uses chlorine to remove zinc, copper, silver, iron, and any other impurities. Finally, the purified gold is ready for sale.

Got Bling?

Some of the most marvelous, famous, and expensive objects in the world have been made of gold. The tombs of Egyptian pharaohs

contained numerous golden treasures. Shipwrecks full of treasure have also been found, including the legendary "ship of gold." This Spanish ship carrying gold and silver from South America sank during a sea battle in 1708 and remained lost for 300 years. Its cargo is estimated to be worth between $4 billion and $17 billion today, though none has been brought to the surface yet. The crown of Charlemagne represented the might of the Holy Roman Empire from the 10th through the 19th century. Now in a museum, it is made of eight panels of 22-karat gold all set with gems.

Nowadays, gold treasures have taken on new forms. In 2014, the auction house Sotheby's sold a gold watch, the Patek Philippe Supercomplication, for $23.9 million. In 2013, a Chinese billionaire hired a jeweler to create a custom

For its historic rarity and high quality, this watch sold for $23.9 million.

iPhone decked out with gold and diamonds. It cost over $15 million. A gold investor in India owns a shirt made of gold lined with velvet. It weighs about six and a half pounds and cost $240,000.

Most gold, however, gets made into jewelry. In the United States and many other countries, a wedding traditionally includes exchanging rings made of gold. In the United States, a bride's wedding band costs between $1,500 and $2,000 on average. While wedding bands symbolize everlasting love, gold jewelry may also represent wealth and success. In the 1980s and 1990s, hip hop stars attempted to outdo each other with outrageously large and expensive gold chains, rings, earrings, and even grills—gold and diamond-covered teeth. This kicked off a trend in gold adornment as fans emulated the stars. Even as trends in gold jewelry come and go, the metal itself is never out of fashion.

Medical Gold

Jewelers aren't the only ones using lots of gold. Dentists also need the precious metal. Since gold is soft yet durable, nontoxic, and doesn't corrode, it makes a great material for forming false teeth or

Au 79
Gold

fillings. In 700 BCE, the Etruscan people, who lived in what is now Italy, made the first known false teeth. Animal teeth were attached onto a gold band that held the teeth in place in the mouth. By the nineteenth century, gold was being used to fill cavities or form false teeth, and gold or gold alloys remain a popular option in dentistry to this day. In some time periods and parts of the world, gold teeth have even become stylish. However, the gold is very expensive. In the 19th century, cheaper options included tin, silver, or a mixture of tin, silver, mercury, and copper in place of gold. Mercury was poisonous, though, and caused health problems. Today, porcelain or plastic-like composites are good alternatives that mimic the color of real teeth, but they are not as durable as gold alloys.

Various uses for gold

Gold is also a key ingredient in two medications for arthritis. Each medication is actually a compound containing gold combined with other elements in a complex molecule. Patients take gold sodium thiomalate as a weekly or monthly injection. The other compound, auranofin, can be taken by mouth.

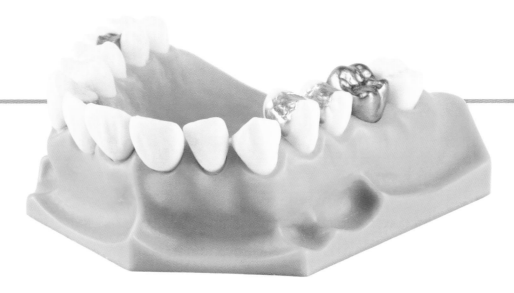

Though used today less than in earlier times, gold can be a useful dental filling.

Doctors first discovered that gold could treat arthritis in 1927. By the 1960s, it became a common treatment option. However, both compounds have problematic side effects, so doctors typically save gold as the last resort when other treatment options aren't working.

One isotope of gold can help treat cancer. Gold has many isotopes, or variations of the element, each with a different number of neutrons in the nucleus. However, just one form of gold, the isotope gold-197, occurs naturally. Gold-198 is radioactive, meaning that its atoms decay over time, emitting **radiation**. Radiation treatments with gold-198 can treat or even cure cancer of the prostate, bladder, or cervix.

Unfortunately, chemotherapy is rough on the body and has many unpleasant side effects. Researchers have started focusing on nanoparticles of gold-198 as a safer alternative. In a 2012 study,

researchers combined gold nanoparticles with a compound from tea leaves in order to target cancerous tumors more directly. In a press release from the University of Missouri-Columbia, physicist Kattesh Katti said, "When we combined the tea compound with radioactive gold nanoparticles, the tea compound helped 'deliver' the nanoparticles to the site of the tumors and the nanoparticles destroyed the tumor cells very efficiently."

Gold nanoparticles also show promise in helping doctors diagnose diseases more quickly and easily. A solution containing these tiny specks of gold will change color if the nanoparticles alter in shape or size. So researchers have come up with techniques that cause gold nanoparticles to clump together in the presence of specific diseases, such as in the infectious blood disease malaria. A doctor working in a remote location can apply a single

Nanoparticles are too small to photograph, but this illustration shows how they might look.

drop of blood to a test strip, then watch for a color change to find out if the patient has malaria.

Golden Nanotechnology

The benefits of gold nanoparticles extend to technology as well. The ease with which gold nanoparticles change color makes them an excellent choice for almost any sensor application. For example, they have been used to make sure that food meets religious guidelines that forbid the consumption of pork. Other properties of gold nanoparticles can be exploited to detect specific proteins, molecules, or pollutants.

Gold nanoparticles can also function as a **catalyst**, or a material that speeds up a chemical reaction. They are especially effective at turning poisonous **carbon monoxide** into the safer gas carbon dioxide. For this reason, some Japanese firefighter helmets use gold nanoparticles to reduce exposure to carbon monoxide, a serious danger inside a burning building.

Carbon monoxide also causes problems in fuel cells. A fuel cell is a battery-like device that produces electricity through chemical

reactions. Most fuel cells combine hydrogen gas with oxygen from the air to produce electricity, with water as the only by-product. Fuel cells could be an important component of a clean energy future. However, the hydrogen gas that feeds a fuel cell isn't always pure. Gold nanoparticles could help remove carbon monoxide contamination from hydrogen, making the fuel cell work more efficiently.

These nanoparticles can also help remove carbon monoxide and

Solar cells partly covered with gold will play a huge role in future energy use.

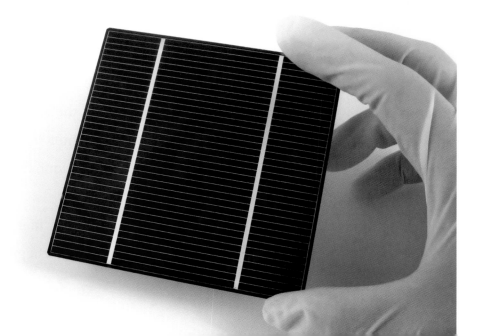

other toxic chemicals from vehicle exhaust. All modern cars that run on gasoline or diesel use a device called a catalytic converter to clean dangerous fumes from engine exhaust. While most catalytic converters rely on platinum, palladium, or rhodium, some are starting to incorporate gold as well. This actually reduces the cost of the converter, since platinum and rhodium are both more rare and more costly than gold.

Gold nanoparticles can also make **solar cells** more efficient. And they are becoming increasingly important in electronics as computer chips get smaller and smaller. Gold nanoparticles allow engineers to print electronic components onto minuscule computer chips.

Gold in Space

Many people love the glimmer and shine of gold jewelry. Gold shines because it reflects light and heat so effectively. In fact, it reflects both **infrared** and **ultraviolet** radiation, while absorbing a large amount of visible light. And of course, gold doesn't corrode and is very malleable, so it's easy to form into coatings or thin sheets. In outer space, radiation is a constant danger. Earth's atmosphere isn't

Au 79

Gold

When Money Grows on Trees

Gold occurs naturally in soil, especially in areas above underground gold deposits. Some plants growing in this soil end up drawing in particles of gold through their roots. Scientists could test leaves of plants for gold in order to find previously undiscovered deposits of the metal. Or, they could try to mine gold directly from the plants themselves. A technique called phytomining uses growing plants as a kind of filter to remove gold and other metals from soil. While it has proven difficult to get the gold out of plants, phytomining is also useful for cleaning polluted soil at mining sites. Chris Anderson is a phytomining expert at Massey University in New Zealand. He was quoted in an article on LiveScience: "If we can generate revenue by cropping gold while remediating the soil, then that is a good outcome."

there to stop harmful rays, so spacecraft components require protection. In many cases, aluminum will reflect away enough radiation. But some equipment requires a touch of gold.

The visor on an astronaut's helmet, for example, is coated with a thin layer of gold. This filters out harmful radiation from the sun while letting in visible light. Some satellites use gold-coated sheets to ward off heat from the sun. The James Webb Space Telescope is scheduled to launch in the fall of 2018, as a successor to the Hubble telescope. It contains a large mirror made up of 18 hexagonal segments, each about the size of a coffee table. A thin film of gold covers each segment. It will help the telescope capture infrared light.

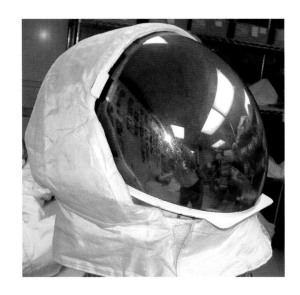

Edwin Aldrin wore this gold-visored helmet when he visited the Moon in 1969.

Au 79

Gold

Shoppers around the world will always want to see their golden dreams come true.

Clearly, there's much more to gold than just beauty and monetary value. Gold is the metal of kings and alchemists, engineers and electricians, hip-hop stars and luxury restaurants. It is the medium of international transactions and an important ingredient in many cutting-edge technologies. Almost all of the gold that has been mined and shaped since antiquity is still around today. It's either been melted down and reused, or has found a home in a museum or personal collection. It's impossible to imagine a world without gold.

 Text-Dependent Questions

1. What industry uses the most gold?

2. Why is the fact that gold nanoparticles change color easily useful in medicine and engineering?

3. What properties of gold make it so useful for outer space applications?

Research Project

Gold treasures come in many shapes and sizes. Choose a gold treasure mentioned in this chapter, or choose your own from online research. Describe what the treasure is, where and when it was made, and for what purpose. Why do you think gold was the material of choice for this particular treasure?

Au 79
Gold

FIND OUT MORE

Books

Ball, Phillip. *The Ingredients: A Guided Tour of the Elements.*
New York: Oxford University Press, 2002.

Bernstein, Peter L. *The Power of Gold: The History of an Obsession.*
New York: John Wiley & Sons, 2000.

Challoner, Jack. *The Elements: The New Guide to the Building Blocks of the Universe.* London: Carlton Books, 2012.

Newton, David E. *Chemical Elements, Vol. 2, G-O.* Detroit, Michigan: Gale Cengage Learning, 2010.

Websites

www.gold.org/

Learn all about the gold industry, gold mining, gold in technology, and more on this website.

www.amnh.org/exhibitions/gold

The American Museum of Natural History held an exhibit on gold from 2006–2007

www.ancient.eu/gold/

Discover gold's importance to antiquity on the Ancient History Encyclopedia.

www.telegraph.co.uk/men/the-filter/qi/8667421/QI-Quite-interesting-facts-about-gold.html

This article includes a list of intriguing facts about gold.

SERIES GLOSSARY OF KEY TERMS

carbohydrates a group of organic compounds including sugars, starches, and fiber

conductivity the ability of a substance for heat or electricity to pass through it

inert unable to bond with other matter

ion an atom with an electrical charge due to the loss or gain of an electron

isotope an atom of a specific element that has a different number of neutrons; it has the same atomic number but a different mass

nuclear fission process by which a nucleus is split into smaller parts releasing massive amounts of energy

nuclear fusion process by which two atomic nuclei combine to form a heavier element while releasing energy

organic compound a chemical compound in which one or more atoms of carbon are linked to atoms of other elements (most commonly hydrogen, oxygen, or nitrogen)

solubility the ability of a substance to dissolve in a liquid

spectrum the range of electromagnetic radiation with respect to its wavelength or frequency; can sometimes be observed by characteristic colors or light

INDEX

Photo Credits

Adobe Images: JPS 20b, Cascoly2 26, Hamsterman 28, Jeffrey Daly 49, Alberto Lozano-Nieto 56. Dreamstime.com: Dibrova 7, kacpura 12, Helena Bilkova 16, Shaiith 17, DVMS 20, Elen 22, Tyrone Cass 24, Thomas Lammeyer 31, Ploychan Lompong 32, Anthony Berenyi 46, Luis Alvarenga 53, typhoonski 60. Flickr: William Boncher 38, Xeric 44. Gotteborg Univ.: 54. Metalworking World Magazine: 58. Patek Phillipe: 50. Project Gutenberg: 15. NASA: 10, 59. Wikimedia: 23, 40, 41

About the Author

Kathryn Hulick started writing about science after returning from two years teaching English in the Peace Corps in Kyrgyzstan. She now lives in Massachusetts with her husband and son. They like to hike, read, cook, visit the ocean, and play with their dog, Maya. Hulick has written numerous books and articles for children and young adults, about everything from outer space to video games. Learn more on her website: http://kathrynhulick.com.